CAN YOU SEE THE REAL ME?

Rebuilding the Real You

KLNelson

ISBN 979-8-89838-597-2 (paperback)
ISBN 979-8-89838-598-9 (hardcover)
ISBN 979-8-89838-599-6 (digital)

Christian Faith Publishing
Meadville, PA
www.christianfaithpublishing.com

Printed in the United States of America

CHAPTER 1

—⚬⟋⟋⟋⟍⚬—

How many times have you heard yourself say, "If I knew then what I know now" or "If I could go back in time"? Maybe the answer is not to be given the chance to go back or the knowledge to know things ahead of time but, instead, to realize that we are all afforded the ability to see where we went wrong, to review the missteps we have taken, and we are all given the opportunity to make things right.

As a little girl, life seemed perfect, like nothing in the world could have been better than the life I was living; and of course, it was. I had no serious responsibilities to manage. My parents paid the bills, took care of our home, maintained our vehicles, and purchased all my food, clothes, and any other necessities. I had no worries and absolutely no stress in my little world.

As a teenager, my biggest concerns were what to wear, getting my schoolwork done, and achieving good grades. Of course, boys were on my mind as well, but again very little responsibility was bestowed upon me. Isn't it funny how we all cannot wait to grow up so we can do whatever we want, we can stay up as late as we want, go wherever we choose to, and behave in whatever way suits us? It is not until we get there that we realize it is not as great as it seemed. We suddenly begin to understand that being an adult is not all the fun we imagined it would be.

We begin to wish we could be a child again and enjoy all the benefits of childhood that we took for granted the first time. We look back and see the person we once were, and we form regrets. We start to wish we could go back, make ourselves more confident, be nicer to others, make wiser decisions, resist peer pressure, get better grades, and just make better choices in general. It is a nice thought, but it cannot happen, and it is not supposed to.

The reality is that we are blessed with one life to live and the freedom to choose how we will live it. We are provided with the opportunity to decide what kind of person we will be and how we will be remembered when we are gone. We are given the amazing ability to make every choice on our path in life and to be the designer of the life we want to have and the kind of human being we want to be in this world.

From the beginning of our lives, we have been given these choices to make, and the decision was always ours. We made ourselves who we are today. Every choice we made molded us for the life we live right now. We are who we designed ourselves to be by the choices we make.

One of our most important choices comes toward the end of high school when we determine a career path for ourselves. This decision decides a lifestyle, invokes a passage to a way of life for us, and determines whether our next set of choices will take place or not.

Finding ourselves in love and making the commitment to spend our lives with someone forms another change of direction in our lives. We are now making choices in our lives, not just for ourselves but for one another and as one united. We must learn to adjust to a second perspective on how our life should be spent and what direction to take. We become enveloped in making each other happy, in finding compromise with one another, and in seeing each other's side of things. This is called upholding our vows.

As a newlywed under the eyes of the Lord, we may be given the blessing of bringing a new life into the world; and once again, our direction changes, and our perspective shifts. We must now make choices that are not only acceptable for our lives but also considerate of the impact they will have on our child's or children's life.

There will always be happenings that occur along the way that curve our path and cause us to change direction, to recreate who we are, with death being the most certain and yet the most unpredictable of those. Losing someone we value in our lives can have the greatest impact on the direction we are headed, and this, more often than not, takes place at the very moment of its occurrence.

There are always a few detours along the way in life; a series of redirection is inevitable. The important thing to remember is that we are in control of the direction we choose and the detours we allow ourselves to take.

The most vital concept we must come to understand is that throughout all of our choices in life and along every inch of the path we choose for ourselves, the Lord has a true purpose and direction for each one of us.

It is when we have found our greatest happiness and most profound peace with the life we are living that we can truly know that we are living the life that the Lord has chosen for us.

As a young girl, I always believed I knew exactly how I wanted my life to be, who I wanted to become, and what lifestyle I would be living. I planned to be a nurse, get married, have four children—two boys and two girls. I was planning to have a big beautiful home that screamed luxury. My husband and I would grow old together, become grandparents, with a home large enough for everyone to come home for the holidays with their loved ones and their babies. My life was going to be everything I dreamed it would be, except not everything that I dreamed of became a reality.

My life did not go the way I always believed it would. The choices I made changed my direction. One very important decision I made at eighteen was to drop out of college. I chose my boyfriend over myself. I wanted to be with him all the time. School did not seem as important to me as he did. This would be my first detour. Life does not always go as planned, and sometimes you get in your own way and lose your direction toward your perfect path, causing your own disturbances, but it is all in how you manage those moments that decides who you are and enables your character as a person to be built.

I did become a nurse. I did get married, and I do have four children, just not all in the order I perceived these moments would take place. I married young at twenty years old. I went back to school and became a nurse after all my boys were in school full-time.

I did not get the grand home I dreamed of, but I had a wonderful home all the same. Not a big enough home for my grown children and their families to come and stay on holidays, but a home filled with an abundance of love and full of comfort and happiness, most days.

The greatest of those dreams that will not occur for me is growing old with my children's father and becoming grandparents together. This dream will not occur because I lost my husband unexpectedly when I was forty-seven years old, another bump in my road, this time created by my husband's life choices.

Three of our boys were just starting their careers, and we still had our youngest at home and attending elementary school. This created the greatest shift in both my life and theirs and resulted in some difficult changes in our lives. My boys are amazing and my greatest inspirations. If you have read my other books, you will understand why.

I have spent my entire life adjusting to change and redirection every step of the way. It was not until losing my husband that I made the greatest shift in my life. I chose to stop working as a nurse, but more than that, I began to see a whole new perspective on my life altogether. Just before my husband passed and during the COVID months, I came to the decision that I wanted to start writing, so I started with a blog.

A college professor had read a paper I had submitted for a nursing theory class, and her advice was that I needed to share this with congressmen and senators. She stated that my writing was something I should continue to do and take seriously. She inspired me to do what I am doing today. After my husband passed, I started writing a book that, to my surprise and much to my delight, was published.

Outside of being a mother, I have never found something that makes me happier than writing. I know that I have chosen the right path, the path God has chosen for me. I believe that the Lord sees when it is time to step into your life and to encourage you to take a different path.

My faith tells me that this is when He shines His light toward the truest direction for your life—the path you were always meant to take.

After my husband passed, the Lord guided me to an alternate path. He has directed me toward a new journey with a wonderful man whom I have known for many years—a journey that I am hopeful will find us living a long and happy life for the rest of our days here on this earth.

It is not always easy to accept the choices that the Lord has for you and to get past the difficulties you endure and the struggles you run into, but if you have faith, then you know that God will never let you fall, and you will find the greatest strength you could ever imagine.

There comes a day when we all find ourselves sitting there, wondering how we got to where we are right now. Some are thankful and feel pleasantly pleased with the life they are living and others miserable and angry with the way their lives turned out. These are the people wishing for a redo, a chance to start over. There are even those who are not entirely happy with the way their lives turned out but have chosen to accept it for what it is and just appreciate that they have a life to live.

Here is something to think about. None of these people are wrong, and all these people still have the opportunity to change their lives, take a different direction, and choose a new path.

We do not have to remain angry, miserable, or disappointed about the life we are currently living. We always have the ability to change it, but with change, you must be ready to accept the challenges and be prepared to put in the work to make it happen. There will be sacrifices to make, and you will want to give up before you even begin. However, I am here to tell you, if you are persistent and push forward with unwavering determination and faith in the Lord, you will succeed.

You will, without exception, feel the greatest happiness you have ever felt in your entire life. That feeling is your soul finding its perfect connection with God and the life He has chosen for you.

It does not matter what your age is or what stage you are at in your life. The only thing that truly matters is that you are ready and willing to make the change. Sometimes the hardest hits in your life are the very thing that gives you the greatest strength to make it happen.

We must not allow the vision of our world to be determined by what is occurring in it today, but instead, we must be determined to make our vision of the world whatever we want it to be.

The first step is finding your strength.

CHAPTER 2

⟨⸻⟩

How do we find our strength? This is not the strength we gain from lifting weights. This is a strength we must find within ourselves. The kind of strength you find when your child is in trouble, when someone is giving them a hard time, hurting them in some fashion whether it be physical or mental. We, as mothers and fathers, find incredible strength when it comes to defending and protecting our babies. Every one of us has an inner strength just dying to be unleashed, and for some, we have not truly allowed that sort of strength to come out of us. We are afraid of the possible sacrifice, of the consequences, and of the end result. We are worried about not succeeding and being let down, but if we never try, then we are only letting ourselves down.

My inner strength was brought out a few times when it came to my babies, but the greatest of my inner strength became present and really expressed itself after my husband passed away. I was hurt, I was angry, and I was completely lost, but I knew I had to be strong for my boys and for myself. For the first time in my life, I realized that the life I was living was not exactly the life I had always wanted it to be. It was right then, at that very moment in my life, that I understood that I had the authority and the ability to change it and there was no one to challenge my choices.

The greatest source of my strength came from within me—because of myself, my children, and through my faith in the Lord. If you know me or you have read my previous books, you know that my favorite Bible verse is Philippians 4:13: "I can do all things through Christ which strengthens me."

I made the choice to let God lead my way. I handed Him the steering wheel that was directing my life, and I took the biggest leap I have ever taken. Yes, I was scared and unsure. I told myself that I had faith that God would never steer me wrong. I asked the Lord to tell me when I was going the wrong way or making a bad choice and to redirect me toward the right choice and the right way. My children were beside themselves that I had stepped away from my job as a nurse, and I was choosing to just sit and wait for the Lord to give me direction. It was six months before His message came.

I know some of you are thinking, "She was grieving. Her mind was clouded by such a significant loss." But the truth is, from that very moment when I decided to step away from my job, I had never thought more clearly in all my life. I felt such an immense release of pressure, and suddenly my burden was no more. It didn't matter that I would have no money coming in. Somehow, I knew the Lord would see me through. That's when I wrote this blog:

> You know that moment when you are standing at the edge of the road, looking across to the other side, and you think to yourself, "If I could just make it to the center of the road, I would wait there a little while longer, determine just the right time to make my move, and then eventually get myself to the other side"—the destination you are attempting to reach, the goal, if you will, that you are aiming to get to.
>
> While you are standing there, watching all the cars filled with people heading to their own destinations, with their own goal lines, you are contemplating your best time to make your move and consciously take your first steps to the center of the road.
>
> All the while, you are mentally saying to yourself, "Man, there sure are a lot of people in a hurry to reach where they are going. I wonder if once they reach their destination, they will

be happy with their choice or if they are already regretting that they have to be there." Why is it that we have to be anywhere, and why do we head anywhere that we already regret before we are even there?

Wouldn't it be better if we all waited just a little while to determine the best time to make our move, just got ourselves to the center of where we were headed, and then contemplated when, and if, we wanted to complete our journey to where we were planning to be?

Wouldn't it be ideal to make sure that where we are headed is exactly where we want to be? This way, every time we are headed there, we are happy with our choice and cannot wait to get there, and every time we leave there, we can't wait to return.

It just seems to me that we are all in such a huge hurry to get where we are aiming to be that we don't take the time to determine if the path we are taking to get there makes us happy. We spend our whole lives racing to get to where we want to be in life, and we lose sight of what really makes us happy and what really matters in life. We miss an entire lifetime of joy because we spend all our time working to, in all truthfulness, get nowhere greater than where we already were.

Yes, we may have more money and lots of toys and gadgets, property, homes, etc., but do we have happiness, joy, love, and peace in our lives? What we have are all these material things and absolutely no time or energy to enjoy any of them. Our whole life has blown by, and we never stopped to take the time to absorb the world around us and all of its majestic beauty that God has given us, the true gift of life. The absolute greatest reward of them all: the ability to just sit back and feel the gratefulness of being able to live your life and be alive. To take the time to really hear the birds sing, smell the sweet scent of the flowers, and be in love with your partner in life. To enjoy the moments with the children you brought into this world and watch them grow.

I was in the center of the road. I had to stop there because my world stopped for just a moment, while the rest of the world went on bustling past me. As I stood there, watching everyone racing to their destinations, I asked myself, "Are they really living their best life? Are they happy with their choices? Do they realize at all that life is passing them by, and before they know it, they will have missed the opportunity to really fully enjoy it?"

I came to the realization, after my world came to a sudden halt, that I had an opportunity, a gift in front of me to change my destination. I had the choice to stop and take in the world that surrounds me. I had the choice to be thankful for everything the Lord has provided me and to appreciate the true beauty that is all around me. I had been given a blessing among the turmoil occurring in my life to slow down and do everything in this life that I wanted to do.

I don't need excess money or glamorous material items. I don't need a gigantic, fancy home. I need peace in my life, and I want happiness in my heart and soul. So I jumped off the crazy train, and I chose God's train. I chose me. I chose life. I chose the things that make me the happiest in my life—my children, my writing, my peace of mind, and my health. I chose to wake up and see the sunshine, to hear the birds chirping, and to feel the breeze from the trees and smell the sweet grass.

I will not be someone's slave so they can make a greater profit. I will not live my life hating it and resenting that I exist. I will not miss the opportunities to reach all my greatest dreams and desires. That is the greatest part of all. I can choose my destination, I can make my life choices, and I do not have to do anything I do not truly want to do. I don't care about being rich or owning the best in life. I simply want the little things that are really the greatest things in life. I want love, I want happiness, I want solitude.

I want to sit in the water, watch the waves ripple in and the sun glisten across them while the birds chirp and the gentle breeze blows. I want to hold the hand of the one I love, kiss the cheeks of the babies I raised, and smile knowing that I lived my greatest life because I quite simply chose to just live it.

I'm making it to the other side of my road. I'm doing it the way I choose to with a smile on my face and plenty of energy to keep going and enjoying where I am.

I spent six months cleaning and reorganizing my entire house. I planted flowers and a Japanese maple tree to honor my husband. I placed a stepping stone beneath the tree that held words of remembrance of him upon it. I focused on my youngest son and attended every football game, every basketball game, and every track meet he participated in.

I wrote blogs that shared my thoughts on what I was going through every day, and I wrote my first book. I cried almost every day. In my last book, I shared with you the day the robins came, and it was that day when my whole life changed.

It was on that day that I found my greatest strength of all. It was exactly what I needed to know, the answers I needed from my husband and the Lord. They would always be with me. I did not need to concern myself with how I would make it on my own. I needed to focus on being happy, on truly living for me and my children, and my life would be everything I needed it to be. With that kind of unyielding strength, I knew life was still possible for me and I could truly make my dreams a reality.

I was not afraid to take chances. I was not afraid to make sacrifices. I was not afraid to get hurt. The hurt I was experiencing already told me if I were capable of enduring that, I could manage anything else that came my way. I was ready to risk it all, step out on a limb, give it my all, play my hand, and see where the cards would fall.

No one is ever promised anything in life. I know my life will only ever be what I choose to make it. I know that there is going to be some turbulence along this new path I have chosen. I am still going to feel the fear of not reaching the point I dream of getting to in my life, the other side of my road. As a human being, I am always challenged with second-guessing myself and continuing to hold onto my faith, not because I don't believe in the Lord, but because we all expect instant gratification in life.

I know now that life is too short to just let it be what it is. You get one life and every opportunity to make it all that you want it to be. Why would you waste it on giving up, not trying, or worst of all, just accepting what it already is?

I understand that half of my life is over, but there is a whole other half to live. I have the chance to make it the greatest life I ever lived, and I am certainly going to give it my all to do just that.

Finding your strength is not easy. For us as human beings, we seem to find our greatest strength in moments of tragedy or when our lives suddenly seem to be hanging by a thread. We channel our inner strength when we have hit our rock bottom or when we are faced with a challenge that brings out our greatest fear. It is when we suddenly feel as if we have nothing left to fear or no other choice left that we give ourselves the opportunity to find our faith and let our real souls shine.

I cannot presume to know where your inner strength is hidden or what will the reason be for you to choose to let it come out, but I would like to encourage you to take the time to search for it. Give yourself the chance to be able to live free and be the happiest you could ever be. Life is only as hard as you allow it to be. God does not want your life to be hard. He wants it to be filled with purpose and to give you a reason to find your faith and believe in Him.

Our strength is everything we allow it to be. We can't go back and change our past mistakes, but we can dig deep within ourselves and allow ourselves the ability to forgive the person in the past and make new the person who stands before our mirror today, the person we always wanted to be. There is immense strength in forgiveness. God forgives us every time we humble ourselves and ask Him to.

As living innate spirits chosen by God, we are blessed through the will of the Lord to bring new life into this world and provided the ability to find forgiveness within each of us for one another and for ourselves. These are just some of the gifts that are given to us and that enable us to prove ourselves to Him and to learn to lean on Him when we lose our way.

I believe that each new life God graciously brings into ours is bestowed upon us for a reason. As I shared in my last book, each of my boys has given me a gift that enables me to be who I am today, and to each one of them, I humbly ask forgiveness for my faults and imperfections in their lives. Every day is a new day and another stepping stone toward learning to forgive myself for some of the choices I have made throughout my life.

CHAPTER 3

⸻ ⟿ ⸻

Forgiveness takes great strength and fortitude. Forgiving ourselves of our past mistakes is never a simple task. If we are truly honest with ourselves and we openly and honestly feel pain within ourselves for the sins we have committed throughout our lives, only then will we learn to forgive our own trespasses. Even if you allow yourself to accept and forgive, you may never really be able to forget. Some things you just carry as burdens for the rest of your life; however, when you reach for the Lord and ask Him to forgive you, you will find peace within your soul.

Perhaps it is not you who needs your forgiveness. Maybe it is someone else from your past who tortures your soul. Forgiving others for the pain they have caused you can be an even harder task. You may not feel that they deserve your forgiveness, and maybe they don't, but you deserve to be free of the anger and the pain you are holding onto and know that they do not get the opportunity to destroy your entire life because of their actions and the feelings you have for them.

I know this is a sensitive subject and one most people do not want to focus on, but you cannot begin to find yourself and live the life you really deserve if you have not found a way to let go and move on.

The Bible tells us in Matthew 6:14–15, "For if ye forgive men their trespasses, your heavenly Father will also forgive you: But if ye forgive not men their trespasses, neither will your Father forgive your trespasses."

I know I made many mistakes in my past that I am not proud of, and there are some that I will feel remorse over for the rest of my days, but I have asked the Lord for His forgiveness, and I continue to ask Him because, as I said, I am still learning to forgive myself, to let go, and to move on.

Guilt and hatred are two of the worst words and emotions anyone can ever hold. I have always taught my children that *hate* is a horrible word and should never be used lightly. To hate someone is an awful action—one that must come with much consideration before you utter and feel such a disgusting thought.

No one takes great pride in either of those feelings, and no one ever should. We should never take our guilt out on anyone else or anything else, but instead, we need to find a way to learn from our mistakes and correct our behaviors so that we never find ourselves feeling such shame again. It's easy to place blame on someone else for your actions, but attacking someone else will never ease your pain.

Being hurtful to those you love because you can't accept your own guilt only causes more pain in your life and allows misery and self-loathing to exist. I have been in the position of having someone's guilt placed on me, as I am sure most of us have, and it's a horrible feeling when someone blames you for their own behaviors and what resulted from them.

I have taken that kind of treatment for many years, until one day, I said, "No more." I found the strength in me to let those people know that I would never be their scapegoat again and to make them look in the mirror and see who they really were. I held a lot of anger toward those people, and it took me quite some time to get over it. I have recently found it within me to feel for them and what they were dealing with and to not only forgive them but also to ask forgiveness for them.

Learning to find forgiveness within ourselves is vital so that we may find a way to move on and live a full and happy life. We need to find ourselves believing that all is well within our soul. It is then that we will find true forgiveness for who we were and when we will suddenly feel completely free—free from anger, free from pain and shame, free to be a brand-new and better you and me.

We as a society are not great at forgiving one another, at least not with any ease. We tend to be more willing to judge one another without seeing who each of us truly is.

I do not believe any of us are innocent when it comes to acting as judge and jury toward others. It is safe to say that you cannot presume to know who someone is without first getting to know them. Just looking at someone does not give you a full, in-depth picture of who they are.

Most of the time, we do not really even know who we are ourselves. Some of us pride ourselves on being a great judge of character, and perhaps we are, but we can never really know the whole of someone or what made them who they are based on outside appearance, even if they appear sketchy or seem to make you feel uncomfortable or give you a negative vibe. The other side to this scenario and a positive spin on this is that people can change. We can all learn to be better human beings and find a way to redesign who we are.

No one is perfect; none of us were ever meant to be perfect. We are human. We were already flawed from day one, and this is because of Adam and Eve's choices. I'm not sure anyone can or has ever lived an absolutely perfect life, but we can choose to work to make our lives perfect for us. Some will never get there because they quite simply are not willing to make the effort to do what it takes. It is not easy to face all of your demons. It is not easy to see all of your flaws or to accept your past mistakes. It is extremely hard to step away from what seems to be the only way and to allow yourself to let go of what you are doing right now. Let go of the job that merely keeps your life afloat, the way of life you know, and just let God step in and redirect you.

It is a scary move, one that sometimes takes a "hitting your rock bottom" moment to give you the strength to take such a big step, but when you do, when you place your strength and your belief in God and just let go, you will find the greatest joy you have ever felt in your life. I am a living proof of that. Your way of getting there may not be the same way that I got there, but I know God is willing to help us all find our way there if we just have faith in Him.

I am not sitting on piles of money or living a life of luxury, but I do not need to because what I have is far greater than all of that. I have peace. I am filled with the greatest happiness I could ever know, and I am living my absolute best life right now because I'm living.

I'm not working my fingers to the bone. I'm not feeling miserable about what I do. I do not dread where I am headed. I hold no anger toward my past and no hatred for anyone. I have found my greatest strength. I have forgiven myself and those who I felt hurt or burdened by, and I have let go and let God take control of my life.

I am thankful to be able to see the moments in my life that changed my direction—the moments that caused me sorrow and pain and placed me in a position to rethink my life—because they have all brought me to where I am today. They have made me realize that they were all meaningful steps that were there to guide me toward the destination I am at now. They are what has given me the strength and the courage to press on and to make the decision to reach for my greatest dreams and make them all a reality. They are why, after all the anguish and pain I have seen these past few years, I am able to smile so brightly today.

Forgiveness takes courage, strength, and a grateful heart. Forgiveness is a great act and a big step in enabling yourself to move on and to be free. Forgiveness is not an easy task, nor is it an easy thing to give, and there are even times when it is not easy to accept from someone, especially from ourselves. If the Lord can forgive, then there should be no reason that we cannot.

No one wants to live their life filled with bitterness and rage. No one wants to spend their entire life feeling regret and disappointment with themselves. Every one of us has some of this going on within us, and we are exhausting ourselves and wasting our lives holding onto it. We cannot go back and change what has been done, but we can change who we are now and do better, behave better, and become better human beings because of it.

Forgiveness is one of the most difficult steps on the journey to redesigning ourselves, and if we are to get through this, we must first believe in ourselves, have faith in who we are, and know that we are better because of what we have endured and made it through.

Learning to believe in and love yourself, as Whitney Houston sings, is the greatest gift of all.

Retaliation and resentment will never give you solace but instead will make you even more angry at yourself, even more regretful, and your life will never be everything you want it to be. However, forgiveness will give you peace of mind and a wellness within your soul that will allow you to believe in yourself and find your greatest purpose in this life.

> Our Father which art in heaven, hallowed be thy name, thy kingdom, thy will be done on earth as it is in heaven. Give us this day our daily bread and forgive us our debts as we forgive our debtors and lead us not into temptation but deliver us from evil for thine is the kingdom and the power and the glory forever. Amen- (Matthew 6:9–13)

Allowing yourself to believe in someone or something is a process for each of us. It takes time and effort to give freely of yourself and let your heart, soul, and mind fully accept something or someone as a reality you can truly have faith in and hold sacred. We must learn to trust in order to believe, and that is a tough personal battle we all must wage, especially when learning to believe in ourselves.

CHAPTER 4

———❧———

You cannot even begin to think of designing a new you without first believing in yourself. We all hold a certain level of pride in ourselves, and there are some who think very highly of themselves, but believing in yourself is no simple task. You must search deep within yourself, know who you are and what you are capable of, and tell yourself that you can do anything you set your mind to. You must have faith in yourself and believe that you have the strength within you to succeed in whatever it is you desire to achieve. This means that you believe in yourself, you believe in who you are, and you believe in and love the person you are looking at in the mirror right now.

Believing in yourself takes great strength. This strength comes from within you—a strength of mind and a strength from within your heart. This is your will to allow yourself to recognize your worth and to see what you deserve in this life, reach for it, and achieve it. You must believe that you can become and achieve anything you want in life because you have faith in yourself to do so.

It was always easier for me to believe in others and what they were capable of doing. I was always more willing to believe what everyone thought of me and who I was and what I was worth in their eyes. I believed that their opinions mattered more than my own. I was so busy trying to find my worth in everyone else's eyes that I never stopped to find and see my own worth. It took me quite some time to realize my own potential, to see that I had a purpose, that I mattered in this world, and that I had something worth sharing.

I came to understand that I had a voice and that I deserved to be using it and I should be using it. I learned that I matter in this world, and I believe that my purpose is to share my story with others and hopefully help someone out there to perhaps see that they matter too.

I believe in myself because I first believed in the Lord, and I could never believe that He would create something that did not matter in this world.

The one certainty in this life that I hold onto is that the Lord will always love me even when I feel as if no one else does, even when I do not love myself.

Isaiah 41:10 says, "Fear thou not; for I am with thee: be not dismayed; for I am thy God: I will strengthen thee; yea, I will help thee; yea, I will uphold thee with the right hand of my righteousness."

His words remind me that I am never alone and that He will always believe in me. His words encourage me to always believe in myself.

We are human. We will fail, we will feel pain, we will find ourselves feeling let down, frustrated, and defeated at times; but we must remember to keep fighting for ourselves and for those we love. We need to never forget the old saying, "If at first you don't succeed, try, try again." We should never stop believing in ourselves and what we are capable of. We must seek out our purpose in life and do whatever it takes to fulfill it.

Human beings came up with the saying, "Seeing is believing," and you can hold to that, or you can find it within yourself to learn that if you have faith in Him, you can always find reason to believe; and if He believes in your destination, you will get there because it is where you are meant to be.

There will be people who make you question yourself, people who are incapable of believing in something they cannot physically see or personally imagine happening. There will be people in your life who doubt your purpose, who do not believe in the choices you are making for yourself, but you must keep on and prove to them that they are wrong.

There is always someone who will insist that the purpose you believe you are destined to achieve is more work than you can possibly perceive. It may not seem plausible to them, but if you put your mind to it and you are determined to persevere, you can make anything a possibility, and you can succeed.

I had people very close to me who believed in me but were not hesitant in telling me how much work it would be to write a book, the length of time it would take, and even how much more difficult it would be to get it published.

Well, I wrote that first book, and it was published a year later. The book you are reading now is my third book. It is always possible to succeed if you just believe in yourself and you are willing to put in whatever work it takes to make it happen.

I imagine that for someone who does not enjoy writing the way I do, it would seem like a lot of work. Someone who does not see the person I am or know my capabilities when it comes to writing would never be able to perceive that this may not be so difficult for me to achieve, and I may actually love the work it takes to make it happen. They do not understand that my persistence in making this happen is stronger than they could ever imagine.

There were times when I was not so sure myself. I knew how much I wanted to succeed at writing a book and getting it published, but I could see the work ahead of me, and I had some self-doubt. I told myself, "Just write the words first and worry about the rest as it comes," and that is exactly what I did. I shared with the Lord what I wanted to achieve, and I asked for His guidance in seeing me through it. I told Him that I knew if He believed in me, I could believe in myself, and with Him beside me, I knew I could succeed.

There will be moments in your life when you will run into walls of frustration. You may find yourself filled with anger and pain toward those who insist on doubting you and persist in trying to make you doubt yourself. You must know that letting those doubts get the best of you and allowing them to rent space in your mind, heart, and soul will never serve you well. Instead, you must continue to believe in who you are and give them time to find their belief in you.

The Lord affords us an entire lifetime to find our faith in Him, so perhaps we can find the patience long enough to allow someone who does not see the good and the passion within us, who does not have trust and faith in who we are, and who is not so willing to believe in our feelings and actions at face value, to take the time they need to find their own belief in the genuine soul we truly are.

We as human beings always seem to question one another's motives and genuineness. We are quick to accuse others of lying and being deceitful toward us when the truth is we never really give them any opportunity to prove themselves because we never really want to be bothered to take the time; and quite possibly, we were burned before and are just not willing to be burned again.

The problem is that we are neglecting to understand that we are all individually unique, and without giving someone the chance, you can never really know if they are worth believing in. You may find that you have single-handedly shut someone out of your life who just may have been the exact person meant to be in it.

Believing in someone is no easy task and not to be taken lightly, but you must see each person as their own person, and you should give everyone including yourself a fighting chance. The best way to find belief in others is to first learn to believe in yourself. The greatest way is to have faith in the Lord and allow Him to take the wheel and steer your heart in the right direction.

You must believe that every person who has entered your path in life entered for a reason, and if they left, they did so because they had either completed their time with you and the task at hand, or they were never meant to be there in the first place. Believe in your journey, believe in the path you are on in this life, and believe in Him, and you will find your belief in yourself and in every right person who enters your life.

The journey of life is a constant struggle, one of many questions, wrong turns, heartaches, and painful moments; but we continue to learn about ourselves and each other along the way. If we have faith in God, we will know when we are on the right path and when we have connected with the right people along the way.

When we learn to believe in ourselves, to have faith in who we are as human beings, we should find no discomfort in others challenging our character. Instead, we should hold great solitude in knowing that we have nothing to be ashamed of and nothing to be concerned about.

You must believe in yourself, have faith in who you are, and know that you are capable of anything that you set your mind to. Half the battle of succeeding is finding your belief in yourself and the strength within you to see it through. Believing in God and knowing He is by your side through it all is an added bonus and the most rewarding feeling in the world.

I believe in God, and I believe in angels. I believe we are all sent angels to guide us on our chosen path and to lead us in the right direction, but it is up to each one of us to be willing to follow their lead and take the steps they are guiding us toward.

I believe if you are truly willing to listen, you will hear them, and if you are honestly open to believing they are there, you will feel them around you and know that they are showing you the way along your life's journey. I believe we all have many angels who surround us, and they are not all unseeable. They may be that stranger along your path who steps in and takes your hand to carry you through and encourages you to keep on, or that car in front of you driving way too slow but is inadvertently preventing you from getting into an accident that is about to occur a few miles down the road.

There are those in your life who, without any reasonable explanation or clear understanding, you just know are special, those people who give you a warm and comforting feeling every time they are around you. I myself have a dear friend who, I can't explain why, I just know is my angel. I just know he is someone special and that he holds a great deal of importance in my life even though we live many miles apart from each other. He is a significant person in my life, and someday I am sure I will eventually learn why I feel that way, more than just believing what a wonderful person he is.

He, of course, is not my only angel here on earth. I truly believe I have many that surround me, and I absolutely believe every one of you do as well.

Your angels are not the ones you were meant to fall in love with or the beautiful children you gave birth to. They are not necessarily a family member or friend; they may very well be someone you have not even met yet.

Our angels are the ones who present themselves when you least expect it. They are the ones who provide that ray of sunshine when you don't even know you need it. They are the sudden warmth that fills your soul and the abundance of comfort you feel every time you are around them.

They are the ones who are sent to protect you, to redirect you, to give you the cold, hard truth when you are persistent that you don't want to hear it; and they are the ones who always seem to be there in your mind, heart, and soul, reminding you that there are good people on this earth who will always be there for you.

What I believe in may not fit your narrative. You may still be searching for what you truly believe in. I can only share with you that until you are willing to believe in something greater than yourself, you will never know the true sense of believing in you, nor will you be able to fully believe in the abilities you are capable of. You will not be able to understand your full purpose here on earth and you will not feel that true sense of happiness, joy, and peace in your life. You must come to realize what a true gift God has given you, and the absolute beauty He has created that surrounds you every day.

When you come to that place and time in your life where you find yourself ready to make a change, ready to start over, ready to follow your heart and achieve your greatest desires, no matter the risk, you must reach deep within yourself, look in the mirror, and tell yourself, "I believe in you." The next step is believing those words, feeling them with the utmost confidence, then take a knee, look to the heavens, and say, "Lord, I believe in You, and I have faith in You to take control and guide me as I reach for my dreams." All that is left is to follow your heart and give it everything you have.

I know. I was there, I reached that place, and I took those steps; and today I am living my dream. I believe without a shadow of a doubt that God is walking beside me every step of the way. I believe in myself, and I believe in you.

There will be those who seek to destroy your belief in yourself, those including yourself who give you self-doubt and give you reasons to question yourself and your faith. There will be those who are not willing to believe and are sent to test you and your strength, those who are challenging you to find your courage, to prove yourself, to channel your inner strength and stand up for yourself. You must never give them the chance to diminish your faith in the Lord.

You must fight the naysayers, the negative forces, the inner demons, as well as the outside challengers. It will be a never-ending battle until you decide that you will never allow it to permeate your shield of faith in Him and in yourself again.

Stand up! Believe in Him and believe in yourself!

CHAPTER 5

———⟨✦⟩———

There will always be those who express their opinions or doubts about your choices in life, those who only see the level of effort and time it may take to get where you want to be or to succeed at what you want to achieve. They are the naysayers.

You must fight against the naysayers, and you will, if you truly believe in your choices and have faith in yourself to see them through. No one can know or understand your level of commitment or the depths of your persistence when it comes to reaching for your most enthusiastic dreams in life. There is not a single soul who can perceive your feelings toward creating a new you and living out the rest of your life the way you truly desire to, no matter the time and effort it may take to get there.

I could not have ever dreamed that I would be living my dream of writing books, getting them published, and running my own business. The cool whip on top is becoming a freelance writer for the local papers in my town, and the cherry on top is doing all of this while living on the most beautiful body of water that gives me inspiration, with the most amazing man beside me, cheering me on every day.

I had my share of naysayers who challenged me, but I also had some of the greatest inspirations that gave me the drive to see it through. While my children were warning me of the pitfalls, they were also my greatest cheerleaders. I myself was a bit of a naysayer because starting over is always scary and uncomfortable.

My husband wasn't interested in hearing anything about my idea of changing directions. Instead, he wanted me to continue on with the achievement I had already accomplished, being a nurse. I understood that, but at the same time, I was not feeling much reward in my life with that choice. I was disappointed in what the medical field had become and not sure I wanted to be a part of it.

I'm not sure he believed there was time to start over, and I know he was concerned about my ability to earn an income from the endeavor I was considering. I never got the opportunity to prove to him that I could do it, but I am sure he is seeing from paradise above all that I have accomplished so far, and I know he is proud.

Through all the work I have done so far, I have had a great deal of support as well. My family members and friends have continuously cheered me on and shared their feelings of pride in me. One of my biggest supporters is the man I love today. He has not only believed in me every step of the way, but he has also helped me achieve more and graciously given me the time to do so, as well as sharing with me his beautiful home and loving me unconditionally every day. I am so grateful that he and I were directed toward each other by those beautiful angels who surround us.

It goes without saying that the Lord is my greatest supporter and the undeniable reason for my success. I speak with Him every day. He challenges me, and I, of course, challenge Him as well; but I honestly believe He walks beside me through every challenge and every new endeavor. I know He hears me when I speak, and as I speak, I know the words I begin to say to Him are His words back to me. He makes me understand what I need to do by getting me to say it aloud to Him. This may not make sense to you, but I can tell you He has never failed me.

We can't let the naysayers deflate our excitement toward change. We must make them see that they are wrong and in turn be an inspiration for them to see that they, too, can succeed at reaching for their dreams and making them a reality.

It is easy to give up and give in, but it is the most rewarding feeling in the world to fight back, challenge yourself, and succeed. It is the most amazing sensation to prove to others and to yourself that you could do it and to be able to stand back and revel in your incredible success.

I wish my husband had experienced that feeling with his dreams. I wish I could have helped him to succeed in reaching them. I wanted nothing more for him.

I do all of this today for him and my children—to show them that it is possible to live your dream. I will always be grateful for the years we had together and the dreamer he was. He let the world and the naysayers get the better of him, and for that, I refuse to let them get me.

Life will always be a challenge if you let it; however, you can choose the kind of challenge it will be. It can work for you or against you. It is up to you to decide the direction you let it take you. The Lord affords us the ability to choose how our lives will be lived, and He hopes that you will choose to find your faith in Him to guide you through it. I cannot make you believe in Him, but I can tell you that living your life guided by His direction is the greatest way to live. I have never felt more peace in my entire life since the day I gave Him full rein to direct my life.

Fighting the naysayers is not always easy, but with the Lord by your side, you will find the strength to get through it and make your dreams a reality. The naysayers can't see the light at the end of the tunnel because they have lost hope, and they have stopped believing they can get there. My husband used to say that *try* is a three-letter word for no, and "when in doubt, the answer is no." Perhaps that is because you are saying you will try, but you do not believe that you can succeed, and if you have doubt about yourself, you will never be able to achieve anything.

Self-doubt is the most difficult challenge to overcome. When you cannot get outside of your own head and get out of your own way, you become your own worst enemy—someone who is willing to give up before you have even begun. You become your greatest naysayer. Telling yourself that you cannot before you have given yourself the chance to make a true effort at reaching for your greatest desires in life is pretty much the definition of "dead on arrival." Hope is lost before it was ever had.

It is never easy to challenge yourself, and to start over in life is a significant step for anyone, but it is even harder to get the naysayers to believe in your choices if you do not believe in yourself to achieve them. It is up to each one of us to lead our lives the way we choose and to give it our greatest effort to live the life we have always dreamed of. To do this, it requires us to have no doubt in ourselves that we can make it happen.

When we learn to dismiss the naysayers and find it within ourselves to reach our goals, not for the sake of proving them wrong but to simply prove to ourselves that we are worth believing in, it is then that we find our greatest satisfaction in ourselves and our greatest pride in what we are capable of accomplishing.

This is the moment when you realize that you are living your best life. This is when all the self-doubt disappears and you finally understand how great living truly is, and you really begin to see all the true beauty that surrounds you every day.

There is nothing more satisfying than proving your naysayers wrong other than the gratification of proving yourself capable of making your dreams a reality.

There will always be those who challenge us, as well as life's own challenges, and it is up to each one of us to learn how to rise and beat the challenge and be greater than the challenger. God is watching and learning about who we are and how we choose to manage each situation. He sees what gives us strength and what beats us down and how we react to both.

Do we lean on Him and our faith, or do we react carelessly and selfishly? Do we ask for guidance, or do we make choices on our own? Do we stand up and fight for what we want in life, or do we give in and give up, fall on our own sword, and surrender? Do we let the naysayers and the battle get the best of us, or do we act like warriors and win?

I know life can be tough, and I know that some challenges are harder to overcome, and sometimes they seem never-ending, but I believe that God does not give us anything we can't manage. He will always see us through every trial.

We may not enjoy every part of the journey, but we will learn from each step we take along the way. We will learn about the kind of person we really are, the depth of the strength we hold, and how much we can take before we actually break.

We must learn to believe in ourselves and in the Lord and know that with Him beside us, anything is possible.

The naysayers and the devil himself can never win when you have faith in the Lord and faith in yourself.

Sometimes you find yourself so tired of trying, so fed up with making the effort and fighting the good fight. Sometimes you are all out of effort to give, but it is then, right at that very moment, that you must find it within yourself to keep going, to pull in every last bit of strength you have and trudge onward, not because God insists that you do, but because you believe that you can and so does He.

Have you ever asked yourself, "Why is it so easy to just retreat and walk away? Why does it seem so effortless to just give up and give in and let others win?" It is easy and effortless because you do not have to use any physical strength and mental force in just letting go of something or walking away from something. There is no challenge to it. You just quit.

The problem is that quitting will never get you to where you really want to be. Letting go only feels good for the moment, but eventually you start to feel regret, remorse, anger, and shame that you let someone, or something, defeat you.

The reality is that it will just keep happening to you unless you find it within yourself to say no, not this time, and not ever again. You must face the naysayer and brace yourself for the fight. You must rise to the challenge and not cower to it, and you must have faith in yourself and in the Lord that you can win and overcome it all.

We do not have to let the world devour us, but instead, we can let our light shine on the world and know that we are defeating our Goliath one stone at a time.

We are sacrificing ourselves to give others hope that they, too, can take on the world with a little fight and a whole lot of faith.

CHAPTER 6

———⊸※⊸———

Direction, strength, forgiveness, belief, and fighting the naysayers are all important steps in designing the truest form of who you want to be, but the greatest step is sacrifice. What are you willing to sacrifice to make your best life a reality?

Will it be time? Perhaps your salary? Maybe someone in your life who is keeping you down and must go in order for you to believe in yourself and your decision to start over? Quite possibly you may even need to sacrifice yourself, let go of your inhibitions, your denials, and let God in to guide you toward your chosen path and the person you are truly meant to be in this life.

Sacrifice is a scary word and an even scarier thought when you consider the act at hand. As human beings, the idea of giving something up or taking chances that require us to lose a part of ourselves or place us in a position of struggle or pain gives us pause and makes us question whether we should even consider such an action. We are programmed to believe that there is no way that giving something up will make our lives better. How could it? Life is already hard enough; we are barely making it work. So how can taking something away make it better?

The truth is, we are looking at the idea of sacrifice in the wrong light. The right question we should be asking is, "What in our lives is hindering us from living our true purpose and our best life?" The answer is anything that makes you feel resentful about your life, anyone who tells you that you can't, anything that makes you feel dependent on it to live at all.

You see, we are not truly living if we are resentful of the life we live. We are definitely not living for ourselves if we are living through someone else's vision for us. No one in this world is living their best life being dependent on every dime they make and hates the job they do to make that dime.

If there is one thing I realized early on in life, it is that money does not bring you happiness. It brings you a lot of things, material desires, a little fun, sometimes a little peace of mind, and a lot of evil.

It is said in 1 Timothy 6:10, "For the love of money is the root of all evil: which while some coveted after, they have erred from the faith, and pierced themselves through with many sorrows."

I know what you are thinking. Without money, we cannot buy food or pay for the roof over our head, the lights, the gas, and so on. Do not misunderstand me. Of course, there are many reasons that we need money to survive, but that's all it is. We need it to maintain our way of living, not to really truly live. Perhaps my answer requires a more in-depth explanation. We must eat for nourishment to stay healthy; we require a temperature-controlled environment to keep our body's inner core stable, and we need shelter to keep us safe from the elements. All these come at a price to us that requires money.

Living, however, is all in the way you view the term. There is a strong difference between existing and truly living. It isn't until you come to the realization that you have spent most of your life working your tail off to make ends meet, postponed all the things you would like to do, or put off all the things you would like to have, that you suddenly see that life is passing you by and you have spent very little time really enjoying all the wonders that surround you. This is when you begin to understand that every step of your life has been about existing and very little of it has been spent truly living and enjoying your life.

You get one lifetime on this earth. In that time, you spend the first eighteen years learning how to be an adult and survive in this world, the next ten to twenty years making a family and career of your own; and before you know it, you have spent all of your children's lives working, they are suddenly adults, and your life is already half over. This is when you begin to realize what an amazing gift God has given you and that you have never really taken the time to truly enjoy it. You have not ever really lived your life at all. You spent your entire life working so that at seventy years old you could finally enjoy what is left of it.

The final ten to thirty years of your life—if you're lucky—when your body doesn't move as quickly, your mind is not as sharp, and your energy is almost depleted, that is when you finally get to enjoy your life and everything you have worked for. Seriously? Is that when you want to truly start living your best life?

How easy will it be to pull that boat out on the water then or ride that motorcycle down the road? How much fun will it be to take that trip around the world? How easy will it be to get back those childhood years of your babies or your own youthful years?

Will all those years spent at a J.O.B. for the pittance you earned be worth all the lost moments you could have spent enjoying life and spending time with your family? Will it be worth all the seconds, minutes, and hours you could have spent taking in the gloriousness of this earth God provided you? Will it be worth it doing something you resent instead of something you love and wasting all that time?

Not for me. I decided life was just too short to work a job that I resented just because I could make good money at it. I realized I was not happy where I was, and I was missing my son's entire childhood. I made the sacrifice to let go of my good-paying career, let go of my pain and resentment for the loss of my husband and the burden he left me, and let God. I chose to share my sorrow with the Lord. I chose to share my dreams with the Lord, and I chose to believe that the Lord would see me through and guide me to my greatest purpose and my best life, and He did.

You may feel that your sacrifice is to work hard so that your children can live a better life, and that's honorable but not accurate. You can give your children a good life by providing for them, but they will have a wonderful life if you choose to live it with them and not away from them for a bigger house or a new car. They will love you more and be happier if you are happy and enjoying life instead of being angry and resentful, tired, and frustrated every day of their lives. It will serve a greater purpose in all of your lives to sacrifice material things for personal time and sanity.

No child wants to spend every day of their lives with an angry mom or dad or one who is using alcohol or some other method to cure their woes and get through every day of their life. The only sacrifice you are making then is the innocence and preciousness of your babies' childhood and the sanctity of their home.

Ask yourselves how much of your life you are really enjoying. Do you wake up with a smile on your face every day? Do you feel at peace in your mind, body, and soul?

Are you the happiest you have ever been? Are you living your best life? What are you willing to sacrifice to get there?

If you are not sure you have the strength and courage to make a change, are you willing to find it within you to have faith in God to take the lead in the remainder of your life's journey?

If you are not content with your answers, ask them repeatedly until you conclude that you are ready to make a change, until you know with no uncertainty the sacrifice you must make to change your direction in life and start designing the real you.

Nothing about sacrifice is ever easy. God sacrificed His only Son so that we might be able to start over and choose a life through Him, so that we would never perish but have everlasting life.

John 3:16 says, "For God so loved the world, that He gave His only begotten Son, that whosoever believeth in Him shall not perish but have everlasting life."

Jesus was nailed to a cross, spat on, and ridiculed for all of us. If He can endure that, then surely, we can manage to make a sacrifice of our own to find our purpose in life and have a life that fills us with our greatest happiness.

For me, the reality was that I would rather live tight and have less than live angry, tired, and regretful for missing so much of my life and my children's lives working to fill someone else's wallet. I was done managing my life under someone else's direction and their approval. I would no longer live by some company's calendar that decided when I could have time off to spend with my family or to just unwind.

I understood for the first time in my life that my parents and my husband and I were doing it all wrong. My husband passing away at forty-nine years old gave me a sense of redirection. It allowed me to see that life is never certain, and it can be taken from you at any moment. We spent our whole lives putting off all the things we truly wanted to wait for the time when we were certain we could afford it. We postponed trips to places we always wanted to see until the timeline would truly be right for us.

My husband worked for twenty-eight years in a career he truly resented, and he made each one of us feel that resentment along with him. His anger and his frustration with life and what it was dealing him kept him away from us, mentally and physically. I spent most of our children's childhood working and going to college so that I, too, could make more money and work a career that would ultimately keep me away from them even more. Why? What happiness did it really bring us? None.

What we should have been doing was enjoying what we already had. We should have been spending time with our children and giving them a happy home filled with thankfulness and faith. We should have given our anguish and our frustrations to God and let Him guide our way. Instead, my husband is gone, and we never reached our goals in life. We never made those trips, and we never embellished on what we truly wanted.

He always had these five-year plans: "Five years from now, we will take another big step, make another big purchase, reach our dreams." We ran out of time, and we never made it to our desired destination in life together.

We misunderstood what the real sacrifice needed to be. We made selfish decisions, not fruitful ones. We let life steer our direction instead of God. We believed we were sacrificing ourselves by working to support our family and to give our children a good life, but the cold hard fact is that we gave them angry parents, material items they have outgrown, and one less parent who suffered from stress and anger and lost his life way to soon.

Our love for our children was without measure and still is. We raised four amazing men, but each one of them holds some very imperfect memories in their hearts today, and for that, I will always be sorry.

We were so busy focusing on maintaining our lives that we let the burdens of life get the best of us. We enjoyed our family, and we had some wonderful times, but we could have done so much more and made life so much better if we had sacrificed the stupidity and let God show us real serenity. Sacrifice is not as hard as you think, but it does take a certain strength and a willingness to let your guard down, let your insecurities go, and just let God take the wheel.

Just sit down in the middle of your yard, soak in the sun, feel the breeze that surrounds you, listen to the birds sing, let it all go, and ask God to take over from there. Sometimes the right sacrifices make the most wonderful changes. Is it really a sacrifice if you end up gaining a better life for it?

Once you reach that moment in your life when you are ready to make the sacrifice to let go, you will be on your way to new beginnings and the best rejuvenation you have ever known. You will find yourself living the life you always wanted to live and being the person you always wanted to be. It may not be a luxurious and fancy life, but it will be you living free of your anger and your frustrations. You will be able to enjoy all the little things in life and begin to feel the happiest you have ever felt.

CHAPTER 7

O ne of the greatest moments for me was being able to take the time in the morning to sit on my porch and soak in the beautiful day ahead of me while I watched everyone else bustling by on their way to work a job they most likely resented. It was at that moment that I knew without any uncertainty that I had made the greatest decision of my life. I stopped letting the world control my life. I took a good hard look at where I was in life, what the world had done to someone I loved dearly, and how it took his life from me; and I said, "This is where I get off." I asked God for strength and guidance to find my real purpose in life, and I believe He has and still is providing them.

That, my friends, is the greatest rejuvenation you will ever know. I'm sure your idea of rejuvenation is a day at the salon or a good massage, maybe a long weekend off; but trust me, those things are Band-Aids to cover the pain, a temporary fix to get through another week or so. A full and never-ending rejuvenation requires a big step and a great sacrifice. It requires your willingness to surrender to the Lord and let Him show you the way.

I am not in any way trying to convince you to believe in the Lord as I do but to share with you the steps I have taken and how the Lord has helped me change my direction, how He has given me the opportunity to live a better life and allowed me to be the happiest I have ever been. I do not know what the Lord's purpose is for you, and I cannot guarantee whether you will find happiness with His answers, but I do know that the world's answers will never be the right ones because only God truly knows why He created you and what your journey in life was truly meant to be.

I do know what true rejuvenation is because I have personally experienced it. It is the absolute best feeling in the world, and my explanation will never give you the full spectrum of its worth. You must experience this on your own, and trust me, you will know when you do.

Rejuvenation is that feeling when you feel yourself taking that great sigh of relief. When every pressure you have ever felt just melts away. When you find yourself smiling for no real reason at all—just because. When not only is there a smile on your face, but your soul is also smiling, and you feel as if you are getting the chance to start over and make your life everything you wanted it to be.

Rejuvenation is when you finally realize that you are in control of your life and you are deciding how you wish to live it. Just know that only if it's the life God has chosen for you will it then feel like it is right, and only then will you see that you are truly the happiest you have ever believed you could be.

Why is it that we always seem to wait until life is at its worst or some tragic situation occurs before we decide to reach out to a higher power and beg for help? Why does it take such a moment to make us believe that God exists or at least hope He does?

Look around you. How can you even begin to think that the world just happened one day? That all of this heavenly creation around us just one day existed? How can you look at the intricate details of a human being and not believe in a higher power? How can you carry a life inside you, one who comes out so intricately built—feels, thinks, and speaks—and not believe that God exists?

For me, there is just no greater answer. I know my life exists because He chose me. I know that my greatest life only happens through Him because He knows why He chose for me to live on this earth. I know my greatest purpose is to live through Him, and He will show me the way.

I understand. If you are not there yet, that is okay. What you must understand whether you believe in God or not is that the world's choices for you will never be the answer that leads you to the real meaning of living. Rejuvenation comes when you decide what the answers are that give you the greatest tranquility and peace you have ever felt in your life. This is when you feel a rejuvenation that only you can truly know.

Our lives are filled with problems and challenges that present themselves daily, and it is up to us to decide just how much we are willing to take from the world's challenges and how we wish to manage the problems that come our way. Speaking for myself, I can tell you that most of my problems and challenges have come from the places I chose to work at and my insatiable need to constantly prove myself because I was forever seeking someone else's approval to believe in my own worth.

Until the day came when I realized that the only approval I needed to be concerned with was God's and my own. That was my first moment of rejuvenation. I stood up and stepped away from all my frustrations and irritations in life, and I decided to live for myself, not for someone else.

No, it was not easy to step away from a career I worked toward for over twenty-one years and a profession that I believed was exactly what I wanted to be in life. It was most definitely not easy to walk away from a consistent income that I needed to maintain my lifestyle, but it was, without a doubt, necessary. I needed to start completely over in my life and to start making decisions that made me feel happy and free. I needed to choose myself and my children, and I needed to choose God's path for me.

I am still learning to let go and let God. I am human and do tend to get ahead of myself along life's way. There are times when I make choices based on my gut instinct before I stop to ask God what His plan is for me and if my choices are right.

Somewhere along the way, the Lord always lets me know when I need to take a step back and rethink the direction I have chosen, and only then do I begin to understand and realize the right path that is awaiting me. It is then that I feel those sudden sparks of rejuvenation bursting within me, and I know I have found my way back to the path He has designed for me.

Recently I was challenged to decide if I should consider a career in nursing again, and I accepted the challenge and decided that it was a part of the purpose I was meant to achieve in my life. I entertained a new nursing position, but this time I gave them my terms and stipulated that I would only consider their offer if they agreed to my terms. This time my career works for me, and only the Lord and I control the narrative of my life. The rejuvenation of having control over the entirety of my life is without measure and the most incredible feeling in the world. When people see the air of confidence you carry, they find a great deal of respect for you, and knowing that I have God on my side gives me the greatest confidence ever. I got the job and with my terms in place. God is good!

I have also come to another new spark in my life. I have learned that the Lord has blessed me with the opportunity to love someone again and enabled me to feel the strength, courage, and acceptance to propose to this man, and he said yes! I have never felt such amazing happiness and rejuvenation in my life. I am truly blessed, and I am fully aware that the Lord has had a hand in it every step of the way.

"When placed in command, take charge," my husband used to recite to us all, and the day I realized I had full command over my life, I did just that. We all must learn that whatever we feel obligated to in this life holds power over us only if we allow it to. The struggles we endure in this world only happen to us if we perceive them as struggles instead of rising and taking charge. It is time to step up and take control of our world and make it what we want it to be. We need to see this world the way we desire to see it and not how the world expects us to.

There may be a boss at your J.O.B., and they may oversee your work, but they are not the boss that oversees your life. Their control over you is limited to the amount of control you allow them to have. No job or boss is worth your sanity, the entirety of your energy, and the loss of time with your family that you can never get back. Let them see that they have to earn you and your time. Never let them believe that they have the power to destroy your life; never let them think that they hold the key to your livelihood. Make them understand that you do not need them and that without you in their world, they will experience a loss they never want to imagine.

Take back the reins that control your life and give them to God and watch your level of rejuvenation soar beyond the clouds of life and burst into the greatest rays of sunshine you have ever seen and the greatest joy you have ever felt in your life.

Never forget what J.O.B. stands for—just over broke. Is that what you want to waste your life working for? Does that make you feel rejuvenated? Is that worth throwing years of your life away for? I can tell you without any uncertainty that I am not willing to waste my life here on this earth for that. I am not willing to let someone else reap the rewards of my hard work while I mindlessly watch my life go by and wait for my seventies to resent and regret it all.

Right now, at this very moment, stop what you are doing, write down everything you desire to do in this life, and ask yourself, "Will I ever get there, working the way I am now?" Think about the life you are living right now and ask yourself, "Am I happy? Is this my best life? Is this the life I want to live? What will it take to make my life everything I want it to be? What will it take to make me feel rejuvenated and at my greatest peace in life?"

Are you willing to make it happen? Is it worth it for you to make the sacrifices you may need to make to get there? Are you capable of doing what you must do to make your life the greatest it has ever been?

Rejuvenation is not just a word; it is a feeling throughout your mind, soul, and body. It is a "life-changing, mind-blowing redemption of your soul" moment. I am still working on fully completing the level of true rejuvenation I wish to reach in my life. I am not completely sure what level of sacrifice I will need to make to get there, but I know that I am truly willing to make every effort to do whatever it takes to make it happen.

Throughout my life, I have seen one man let the world destroy him and take his life way too soon, and I am watching two men who spent their entire lives working it away, and now all they have to show for it is memory loss, body aches, and pain. It truly breaks my heart, but at the same time, it inspires me to stop and enjoy every bit of my life right now and for the rest of my life from this point forward. I wish that were a lesson I had learned much earlier in my life. There are many things that I wish would continue on with our children today and the world they are living in, but working my life away is not one of them.

You can sit and look back at your life and regret your choices, but do not hold onto them and let them destroy you; instead, choose to do those things you wished you had done before and do them now. At the very least, live your life now the way you always wanted to—right now. Find your rejuvenation and let yourself feel it in your life from this day forward. Let go of your regrets and your resentment, forgive yourself and others, find your faith, believe in yourself, and design the real you, the person you have always wanted to be. Reach the level of peace and happiness in your life you have always wanted to feel.

Have you ever thought about what peace and happiness look like for you? Have you ever believed enough in yourself to think that you deserve to have both of these in your life?

As I am writing this chapter today, I am realizing that I am still working on reaching this point in my life to its complete fullness. Why? Because I still have not come to terms with letting go of people's opinions of me and how people seem to love to tear me down. I am still finding my strength to not let these people get the best of me and to make them see that they will never take from me anything that I do not allow them to. I am still learning just how awesome I am and how amazing I can be if I never let the evilness of others win.

Together I believe you and I can beat the odds and rise up and across our rainbow to the pot of gold on the other side. I believe our road has not come to its end yet, and the path we are on still has a bright light waiting to be found somewhere along this journey of life we are traveling.

I believe we do have a choice in our destination and that we can find the peace and happiness we are searching for along the way.

Rejuvenation is the first of many incredible breaths we take along the way as we realize that we are creating the world we desire to live in and that we are designing the real and true person we always wanted to be.

CHAPTER 8

P eace and happiness are not the mind frame you choose to live in; it's a destination you reach when you suddenly realize that you have everything you have ever wanted in your life and that you no longer feel the need to let other people design your life for you when you have come to the decision that it is no longer okay for anyone else to decide who you are or whether what you do or say is acceptable to them.

True happiness is knowing that only you and the good Lord are directing your life and the path you are on. Too often we live our lives trying to make everyone in it happier than we are, and for a minute, that is where we find our happiness, but when you see that measure of care is not reciprocated by others, you come to understand that there is more to your happiness than just fulfilling others.

As I said before, I found someone to share the rest of my life with, and he fulfills a great deal of my happiness, and he tells me that I do the same for him, but we must still work on fulfilling our own happiness and learning that while we are great at making others happy, it is it is only ourselves that can make our happiness complete.

For too long, we both lived with someone who sucked up all the happiness in the room and was never really concerned about how happy we were but instead more concerned with what we were lacking as a partner. As for myself, I know I have spent my entire life concerning myself with other people's opinions and feelings and letting mine go by the wayside. This is a challenge I am still trying to tackle and one that continues to burden me. As the saying goes, "I am only human," and as a human being, I am prone to fail. The problem is I am only failing myself.

As you work to recreate the person you have become into the person you want to be, think about the kind of life you know without a doubt would make you the happiest you have ever been. However, when you are doing this, do not think of a life you have no means financially to create. Put yourself in a place mentally that you can visually see and physically get to.

For me, that vision is spending every day doing only the things that I want to do, not what someone is telling me I must do to keep what they believe they are providing for me.

My greatest life is one spent on my beach, soaking up the sun, feeling the grains of sand surrounding my toes, and knowing I have no place to be. I only need to just be. Of course, my vision is not me living this life alone. My vision includes the love of my life right beside me, holding my hand and enjoying the scenery we are both taking in as we sit on our beach chairs, hearing the world behind us bustling by, knowing we have no more hustle to give in our lives. This, my friends, is what I call peace, peace of mind, peace in my heart and in my soul. This is the story I want to live, and I hope your story finds you every happiness and peace you can possibly feel.

It is not enough to just envision your perfect life. You must really want it, and you must believe that you deserve every bit of it. Once you believe that you deserve it, you must have faith in the Lord that He will not let you fail in achieving it. As long as you are willing to give Him the reins and to make the sacrifices you need to make to get there, you will most certainly make your way to the other side of your road, where every bit of your happiness and peace lies waiting for you.

One morning, about six months after my late husband passed away, I was driving to work and came to a stoplight. While sitting at this stoplight, I found myself watching the traffic as it passed by and looking at the woman in the car beside me and the man in the truck behind me. I started thinking to myself, "I wonder where all these people are in such a hurry to get to this morning. I wonder if where they are headed is a happy place for them. I wonder if they are living their best life, the life they always dreamed of living." At that very moment, I realized I wasn't. In fact, I came to a sudden realization that I had not been happy for a very long time. I was not living my best life at all. I was living someone else's ideal of what life was supposed to be because it made them happy, or so I thought.

I spent thirty-plus years living a life that I believed was just the way life was supposed to be. Get married, have children, work until retirement, and then if we had made enough, we could truly live out our dreams. I worked diligently to be a good wife and a good mother for almost half of my life, and then suddenly, thirty-plus years later, I stopped at that stoplight, realizing I never thought to ask myself what I wanted. What would make me happy, what kind of life did I want to live, and why was I not living it the way I wanted to? Isn't that what they program you to believe, that when you become an adult, you can do whatever you want to do with your life?

No one ever shared the struggles of working a job or the strife of paying bills. No one ever said, "You have to insist that you will not be programmed to follow the leaders before you. You should want better. You should want more. You can have every bit of the life you want to have, but you must allow yourself to sacrifice what you think you need in life for what you really want in life. Money and material things are fun to have, but they will never bring you the peace and happiness you desire; they will only have you working harder and giving up more of your life to get them.

Peace and happiness do not come from an object or a multitude of items. It comes from within your soul. It is a feeling inside of you that makes your entire soul shine. It's that moment when you feel your smile radiating all the way through you, from your head to your toes. For me, my peace and happiness come in many forms. I feel it when I look at my new love. I feel it when I look at my children. I feel it when I look at my beach, and yes, I even feel it at my new job.

I run the kinship program at my current J.O.B., and for me, it does not feel like a job. I feel the greatest reward in what I do, and this, my friends, is when you know you will never work another day in your life because when what you do is something that you love and you find no level of regret or resentment in it, then you are not working a J.O.B. at all. I am proud of the work I do and honored to do it.

I pray that you find that same level of happiness and peace in your life. I know you can, and I believe in you to be able to get yourself there.

There is not a single reason you cannot find your way to reaching such a fantastic place in your life. The simple fact is that you are the only one who can keep yourself from getting there. Peace is something that comes from letting go of your pain and anger, forgiving yourself and others for things in the past, and relinquishing the reins of your life to the Lord. It comes from determining if the path you are on is filled with light and promise. It starts with coming to terms with whether the people in your life build you up or tear you down and if the work you do is something you absolutely love doing, or you resent and regret every day that you are there.

Are you living your best life? When you look at the people you love, do you feel pride and unyielding happiness? Do you truly believe these people feel the same pride and happiness as you in their lives? Do they believe in you? Do you enter your place of work with a beaming smile on your face every day? Do you feel honor and reward in the work you do? Is your life being spent working and not affording you time with those you love? Are you truly living or just existing?

If most of your answers are no, then you need to rethink your choices, and you need to become the architect of your life and change the blueprints that you started into something you can feel pride in. You need to start over and create the life that brings you the peace and happiness you deserve. You need to begin designing the real you.

Life is too short, and tomorrow is never promised, so you must sit down and answer these questions and start living today for yourself. It is not selfish; it's necessary. You can't give the best of yourself to those you love until you love yourself and the life you are living.

You must find it within you to stop what you are doing, spit in the wind, put your sword out, and fight for the life you truly wish to live. It is time for you to become a warrior and take back your life. No one in this world is going to look at you and say, "Hey, you are not living your best life. Let me wave my magic wand and give that to you." You have to insist on it for yourself and be willing to sacrifice those things that stand in your way of getting there. You have to be willing to see what you must do or be willing to live without to get to that place that gives you the greatest peace and happiness you have ever known.

I'll be honest with you. For some of us, it takes having an immensely impactful moment occur in our life to find the strength we need to get there—the loss of a loved one, a horrible accident, the reaction of someone we love—to incite that we desired change that does not include us. I hope for you it's just reading these words that helps you see that you want more and gives you the momentum to start thinking about what it is going to take to get there.

To be a warrior, you must truly understand what being a warrior means. You must come to terms with and be willing to sacrifice a part of you that right now seems vital to your life. You must dig deep within yourself and find the strength required to do whatever it takes to reach the place in life that you desire to be. Yes, it may impact those close to you, and they may question your choices at this very moment. They won't be able to see the endgame or the reasoning behind your decisions.

You must know that what you are choosing is worth everything to you. You must believe in yourself and the goals you are aiming to achieve. You must be able to see that, in the end, this endeavor will be better for everyone you love because you will finally love yourself and the life you are living.

When you have won all the battles and you have come through them all like a warrior, the reward is incredible. To know that you are filled with this much fight and are bold enough to rage through it and strong enough to make it to the other side, with a sense of pride and all the blessings of the Lord upon you, is the most amazing feeling ever.

Remember that your greatest weapon through each and every battle is having faith in the Lord. He holds the map to your battle plan. Are you ready to be a warrior? Are you ready to feel your greatest peace and happiness?

CHAPTER 9

I t is not every day that you wake up and find that you must learn to fight all of life's battles on your own. It is, however, always a glorious gift the Lord provides us—to be able to take the life we have been blessed with and make it our own. We can choose to give up and give in to the grief-stricken moments, or we can stand up, stand strong, and take back what is left of our lives and start it over.

We can choose to work hard and chase all of our dreams and make our life exactly what we want it to be, if we just first learn to believe and have faith in the Lord.

You see, with hard work and determination, you can succeed and make all of your hopes and dreams a reality. You must first decide not to despise your past but to learn from it and be stronger because of it. Through faith in the Lord and an undeniable willpower, we can all be warriors.

> She awoke to a darkness, an abyss filled with pain, and with one unexpected phone call, she would never live life the same.
>
> As she heard the words spoken, she became frantic and screamed, and she knew at that moment, her worst nightmare had gleamed.
>
> She stood in the doorway, gazed at the terror in her sight and walked to his bedside filled with anguish and fright. Leaning over the bed with tears in her eyes, she kissed his warm cheek and said her final goodbyes.

With pain in her heart and a heavy sigh, she held onto her boys while they prayed, and they cried. The Lord now had his soul with Him. They left the room, and the lights went dim.

Each day she woke up to the morning light, and each evening she tried diligently to sleep throughout the night. With nightmares abound, she wondered how she would ever again feel safe and sound. She could not see the end in sight.

She works hard every day to fulfill her life dreams and make each moment matter. She is determined not to stop and to keep climbing that ladder.

Today she is walking in faith through the Lord's rays of light. This woman is me, and I am a warrior in flight!

This is my story and the parable of my life. What will make you ready to be your own warrior in flight?

We do not come into this world with a set of rules and guidebooks to walk us along every path we take or protect us from the pitfalls that are bound to occur. We are not programmed to know when the pitfalls of life will hit us the hardest. We are not provided certainty on who we will fall in love with or when, and we can never know just how our life story will play out and how it will come to an end.

Every step of our lives is a process of guesswork and hopefulness. One day we suddenly realize we exist on this earth, and our lives are guided for a short while by our parents' choices and their rules. Eventually, we gain the ability to have minds of our own and decide to start making choices for ourselves. We are now deciding what kind of person we want to be, how we want to be perceived in life, and who we are attracted to. We are hopeful that this person we are attracted to feels the same way and that our choice is a good one, one that carries a long, fruitful relationship for years to come. We then begin planning a family, a career, and a life together among all these choices.

Of course, nowhere do we find sidenotes that state, "Watch out for the financial burdens," "Get ready for the risks that come with bearing children and starting careers," "Be prepared for the marital fights over money and differences in opinions," "Are you aware that you are going to start questioning yourself and your choices?" "Did you know that you will let yourself down and others around you?" These scenarios are most certain to happen in almost everyone's lives at some point in time.

It is the very difficult moments that really throw us for a loop, like addiction, health issues, diseases, and of course, freak accidents that no one is ever prepared for in life. Sometimes we are even destined to take on additional responsibilities with no given choice in the matter, and we just do it because we know it is the right thing to do and our hearts would never allow us to say no.

Life is a real battle. The world most days feels like a mastermind of some higher power who is just sitting back, watching you struggle, all the while knowing He is not finished with you yet and the best and worst is yet to come, but you will never know which is going to come first.

While we strive hard in this world to create a great life for ourselves and fight our inner demons, we are always finding ourselves tripping over the efforts and overthinking whether we are doing the best we can and whether we have done enough. We allow stress to control us, and we start to abuse ourselves mentally and physically over things that are not really in our control. All the while, that higher power is keeping watch and waiting for you to ask for His help.

It is at this point in our lives that our choices start to affect our loved ones, and with this comes even greater pain and strife and further abuse of ourselves. It becomes quite a burden to see the anguish on your loved ones' faces and know that you are the cause.

It would seem that everything we worked so hard to accomplish just never seems to pay off and we are destined to just continue to work hard and continue to find ourselves feeling let down by the curses of the evils of the world, but the reality is that we have the ability to change all of this and to most assuredly prevent most, if not all, of this from happening.

No one is ever required to go against their morals or give up on their dreams. All of us just need to be strong enough to stand up for them and fight for what we believe in and what we desire out of this life. Anyone who just goes along for the ride is not really living life; they are just passing through it. You must decide. You have the choice to stand strong and walk with pride or slither along as an empty, defeated shell with absolutely no purpose in your life at all.

As for me, I will stand proud with a backbone of strength, faith, and determination. I will fight for what I believe in and strive for my dreams with my every last breath.

It may not always seem like the ideal choice to step back and walk away from a good job or a mediocre life and start over, but how does it feel to sit back and just accept where you are in life just because it's the easy thing to do? Are you happy? Truly happy? Or are you just willing to put up with where you are because you are not willing to be courageous enough to step out of your comfort zone and put in the effort to strive for the better?

Before I lost my husband, I was working a job that did not really fit me just to appease my husband and be out there working so he didn't have to. After I lost him, I realized this, and I stepped away from that job. I stepped away because it was not where I wanted to be and because I decided I wanted more out of my life. I wanted to find what made me happy and to reach for my dreams.

I concluded that life is short, and you must live it, and live it with the fullest purpose. Why wouldn't you choose to reach for the stars and fight for everything that makes you happiest and feel as if you succeeded? Why wouldn't you want to feel so full inside, feel the reward of knowing that you couldn't possibly ask for anything more out of life, that you are so completely content with everything you have and everyone you have in your life that life couldn't possibly get any better?

That's what I am aiming for. That is my ultimate goal. I know what I want out of this life and who I want to share it with, and I plan to do everything in my power to make that happen. I know what my beliefs are, and I will always stand strong in those beliefs and fight for those beliefs that mean everything to me.

I will not let anyone decide what is right for me. I know there is only one who truly controls my destination and what is right for me, and that is my Lord and Savior Jesus Christ. Through Him, I make my choices in life, and I fight for my desires in this life. He sees to what success I have in achieving my life's desires. I have faith that He will never let me fall. I know that I can do all things through Him and with the strength He provides me.

So as you are sitting there today, at home or at your job or wherever you may be, ask yourself, "Am I happy? Do I have everything I ever dreamed of? Does my life feel full enough for me? Am I content with what I have, and does it fulfill my every desire?" If you know that you couldn't possibly be happier with your life, then good for you. You did it. If you find that you just can't wait for the day to be over, and you have desires that you have always wanted but feel they are so far out of reach for you, don't give up. Don't let go of those aspirations. Tell yourself that you can have them, that you are worth the effort, and push yourself to achieve them.

Ask yourself, "Will I leave this earth knowing I had the best life I could have asked for? Will I feel as if I could not have asked for anything more, or will I take my last breath wishing I had reached for that dream job, fought to make that one person mine, and achieved those ultimate desires I always wanted?"

I know that I don't want to spend my last days on this earth wishing I had done more and changed course. I don't want to resent myself for not trying harder and giving it everything I had to achieve all my dreams. I know for certain that I don't want to spend my last days alone and wish that I reached out and made every attempt to be with the one person I believed would make the rest of my days full of happiness and love. I know that God's plan has guided me to the man who is meant to share the rest of my days here on earth with me, and how blessed I am to have had two perfect loves in one life.

I have always told my children to find what makes them happy and don't make what they do a job; make it a joy—a place you look forward to being and that fills you with reward in your heart and gives you the desire to want to be passionate about what you are doing. We can all work a J.O.B. (just over broke) position, but how many of us are willing to make the effort to work a dream?

I am not going to give up, and I will never give in to another's ideals for me or what they believe is right for me in this world. This is my life, and I will choose my destination.

I will fight against all the wrong ideas out there, the ideas that go against the very nature of the good Lord's scripture and commandments because a corrupt nature is an evil one. We should all want a better world—not one that suits our convenience but one that holds beauty and love for one another and finds us living with one another with respect and appreciation, lifting one another up, not tearing one another down, and saving lives, not destroying them for our own greed and desires.

The Lord has blessed my life many times already, and I will continue to glorify Him and fight to make my life everything I want it to be and to hopefully hold everyone I want in it.

I hope that you will look within yourself and determine if you have found success, not just in a career but in yourself and your life. I hope on your last days, your heart is full and your mind at ease because you know you could never have been happier in the life you lived.

I wish you all God's blessings and the best life can offer. I wish for you to be the warrior who makes your life everything it was meant to be.

If the world were perfect, what would we have to look forward to? If the sun were always shining, how would we ever see the stars? If everything were just given to us, what would we have to fight for? What would inspire us to aim higher or want more? If life were perfect and easy and everything we wanted just came about freely, would you be happy?

Have you ever thought about what life would be like without having challenges in it? Would it be simple and perfect, or would it be boring and dull? Almost certainly it would be whatever you perceive it to be.

What would it be like if the sun never went down and the world was always full of light? Would we tire of the brightness and yearn for the dark, or would it just be what it is, and we would just learn to adjust to never seeing the night, the moon, and the stars?

How would our life be if we all were without emotion, no feeling of sadness, happiness, anger, or love, would life even be worth living?

Do you ever wonder if God thought of all these things before He created the heaven and the earth and all of us humans? It would seem that He must have. How else would all these things that we take for granted exist in our everyday lives? How would we appreciate anything in our lives or each other without feelings?

What an incredible position God was in to be able to not only create a landscape and all the fillers within it but also be able to decide all the intricate details that make everything work around us and those details that make up all of us as human beings and provide us with the ability to see, hear, smell, touch, and emotionally feel. Humans alone are filled with such detail and hold such amazing workings within them, and still He created all of us and all the beauty that surrounds us, all in seven days. What a glorious designer He is!

I only wonder, What would it be like to feel no pain? To never suffer, to never feel heartache, depression, or disappointment? I know that is the price we must pay for Adam and Eve's choices those first few days, and I believe that is why He gave us the ability to show emotions and feel emotions because we cannot only feel pain, but we can also feel comfort and give comfort. We cannot only feel heartache, but we can also feel love and give love. We cannot only feel depression and disappointment, but we also feel enlightened and give praise and encouragement. We cannot only feel suffering, but we can also feel blessings and joy. He matched every painful emotion with a positive, delightful emotion.

He gives us the ability to choose our response to every occurrence in life. We can decide how we respond to all the negative emotions and how we carry on. We get to decide how we will live our lives, how we want to feel, and what will make us happy every day. What an incredible gift!

God did not make us to be one certain way. We make ourselves who we are and the person we portray throughout our lives. We decide our destiny and the kind of life we want to live.

God did not create evil; we as humans did that to ourselves. Wouldn't it be nice if we were all positive creatures and shared kindness every day instead of hatred and disregard for each other and our world?

Look around you, take in the beauty that surrounds you every day, and remember that God gave you everything you need and more. Life is what you make it and what you want from it, so if you know what will make you happy, reach for it, and make it happen. No matter how hard the goal may seem or how long the journey may be, just go for it. We are only meant to live on this earth for a short time. Don't waste it being sad and angry, lonely, and hateful. Find your happiness and just grab it! Once you have it, thank God for giving you the ability to go after it and make it happen! This is when living your best life begins.

Be a warrior!

CHAPTER 10

—◦◦◦◦◦—

Stop telling yourself it can wait until tomorrow. It is never okay to wait another day. You never know what tomorrow brings. Sometimes we believe we need time to figure things out or to make a secure decision, but the reality is that time is not on our side. Life is short, and there are just some things that shouldn't need time for you to figure out. There are times when you should just know; you should just be able to feel that something is right. If you feel like you are ready to burst inside like nothing could seem more perfect, then it is worth the risk, and you do not need to take the time to think things over before deciding whether it is ultimately everything you have ever wanted in your life.

Why can't we just say, "This is what I want, and I will not settle for anything less"? Why can't we just hold out for everything we have ever desired in our lives and wait for it to happen? I know I am on two different sides of the spectrum right now.

On one hand, I am saying life is too short to take the time to think things out, and on the other hand, I am saying hold out for your dreams; don't settle for anything less. Both sides seem right to me. I decided to hold out for my dreams. I do not wish to take on a job just to have a job. I want to be happy with my job. I want it to make me feel completely fulfilled and proud. I want to look forward to going to work every day and know that I am succeeding and accomplishing something great.

It seems we live in a world where we are all just running around in chaos. We live in a world where we have way too many options to choose from, and we seem to want even more. I think all of us have forgotten how nice it is to just simply live. I think we are all missing what is important in this life and way too busy trying to have more, striving for better, so much so that we may just be missing what is already in front of us, and it may very well be perfect for us.

The point here is to stop making everything a drawn-out deliberation and just know what you are looking for and what you want out of life and make it happen. Reach out and just grab it before it is too late, before life gets away from you and you never find those moments again. Fight for your dreams and follow your feelings and your instincts. Take control of your life and make it everything you want it to be.

There is no better time than the present to see all of your dreams come true. We get one life, and we are never guaranteed how long we get to live it, so live it. Do not procrastinate and put things off to a tomorrow that you may never see.

I know it all seems a bit silly and unrealistic, but I have seen what procrastination and time does. I listened to my husband say, "We can't do that right now. We do not have the money, and it is not the right time." Well, folks, the right time took too long, and my husband passed away without warning and never fulfilled his dreams. He never saw the places he wanted to see, and his life ended unexpectedly without ever getting there.

So if you are telling yourself, "I'll get there someday" or "There is plenty of time," if you are thinking you just need time to decide whether something is right for you or if you are sure that you are making the right choice, don't wait because you never know if someday will come, and you can never know how much time you really have.

Get out there and enjoy your life; grab onto the ones that make you feel on top of the world and never let go. Keep living for today and be thankful for every tomorrow.

A Shakespeare play first quoted, "The world is your oyster," meaning that everything is open to you for you to take the world and make it what you wish it to be for you. Well, that metaphor is not so present today. The world is open to whatever you want from it as long as the government does not succeed in taking away your very freedoms that give you the ability to reach for the things you want to make your life what you want it to be.

I have spent my entire life fighting for everything I want in this world, and I will never be done fighting. I have always raised and taught my boys to stand up and fight for what they believe in and what fulfills their happiness. My late husband and I taught them to be men and not to be afraid of confrontation or a challenge and to battle through the hard times, to never let the tough moments beat them. Everything in life that matters to you is worth fighting for, and I still believe this. So I am still fighting! I am standing strong for my beliefs in this world, and I will not let a government body decide what is best for me. I will not sit by and let the challenges that confront me decide where the direction of my life is headed.

I will succeed in my career, in my life choices, in my happiness, and in love. I succeeded in all these before, and now my challenge is to start over again and to succeed in what I want for myself and the rest of my life! Now my life will be centered around me. I know this sounds arrogant and selfish, but I spent thirty-two years of my life centered around my husband and twenty-nine years centered around my children; and yes, I will always focus on my children as they are my life, but I must focus on myself too.

It is time to lead by example for my children and show them that Mom will never stop fighting and Mom will succeed and find all the happiness she deserves in life. This allows my children to see that they should never give up and never give in and they should always stand strong in every battle in life for what they desire out of it!

I have raised real men in a world that challenges that quality in men every day, and I will never allow my men to be anything less than that. This does not mean they cannot have emotions and feel and cry when things hurt or that they are any less of a man for respecting a woman and being compassionate to her needs. It does mean that they should never allow a woman to walk all over them and take from them the very strength that has been instilled in them.

This does mean that they should in turn raise strong men, real men, passionate men, respectful men, and loving men; and they should raise strong women with the same qualities, who love themselves, love their children and their spouses, and love their country and their freedom.

The challenge is to be a person who will never let anybody destroy your hopes, dreams, desires, and your person, simply because you were not willing to stand up to the challenge and found it easier to just give in to defeat.

The challenge is knowing that we have one purpose in this life— to live it to the fullest and to live it the way God would expect of us. We get one life, and it is never a guarantee that we can live a long life, so we must stand for our happiness now and teach our children to do the same, or we may very well find that we just let life and everything that could be great in it pass us by, that we allowed ourselves to never feel true happiness, true success, true love, and true satisfaction for a job well done raising amazing children who we know will survive and survive well. Is this what we want to realize when our time to leave this earth and enter those precious gates of paradise comes?

Folks, don't let anything in this world stop you from finding your true happiness, success, love, and satisfaction in a job well done. Stand up and be strong; fight for your happiness and for your children's happiness. They are counting on us to lead by example and guide them into fighting for their happiness, freedoms, success, love, and satisfaction in a job well done raising their own children one day!

Have you ever looked among the flow of traffic on your morning commute? It would seem that everyone is moving in the same direction, but the truth is that almost everyone on that road will not be arriving at the same destination or even continue on the same route. Instead, each one will choose their own unique path and pattern to reach their previously decided point of interest.

We, as people, say things like, "He is just like his father," or "She looks just like her mother." The reality is that they may hold physical characteristics and even personality traits of their parents, but they are their own individual persons.

Your son may have your husband's eyes and maybe even his smile. He may have a short fuse just like you, but he will always be who he chooses to be, beyond the person that his mother and father are.

We as a society may all be heading somewhere at the same time of the day, but it does not mean that we all are heading to a job. If you look around the crowd that surrounds you on the road you are traveling, everyone seems to be focused to get somewhere, but we can never know just what is going on in each person's life at that very moment, or what kind of life they have endured up until that point. You may be headed to work; the guy beside you may be headed to a funeral for a loved one, and the woman behind you may be headed to a shelter after being abused all night by someone she believed loved her.

When you arrive at your planned destination, do you look around and people-watch? Do you look over at the guy with a disgruntled look on his face and think, "What a jerk"? Do you look over at the woman struggling with two children and say to yourself, "She really needs to take control of those kids"? How could you know that the guy you assumed was a jerk by the look on his face was holding that face because he hadn't slept in the last forty-eight hours because he worked a double shift for the last two days, or that the woman you believed to be a weak mom with no control of her babies is actually a single mom, who works nights and is trying to run her errands during the day to make sure all her bills get paid to keep the lights and water on for her children?

My point is this: We all may be headed in the same direction, but we all hold a different purpose in this life, and each one of us holds a different pattern of genetics, behaviors, goals, and ethics. Each one of us is going through our own trials and tribulations in this life. Your son may look like his father, but he will never be the exact same person as his father. Your daughter may smile like her mother, but she will be forever smiling for different reasons than her mother, and her smile will be presented based on her personality and her personal emotions. Her reaction to a bad day will be different from yours, and the way she loves may be similar, but she will find her own way of accepting love in return.

Each one of us must remember that the toughest critic we have is the one in the mirror. The biggest challenge we will endure is the one we give to ourselves. The greatest pain is caused by our own acceptance of it. We are our strongest warrior and the central puzzle piece that completes the desired picture of the life we are working toward.

We are all on our own path designed by God to reach the destination He has chosen for us. Along the way, we are fighting through our own individual struggles and trudging through our own turmoil that, through our own personal choices, we have created for ourselves. So you may have his smile; you may look in the mirror and see his face in some fashion, but you must remember you decide where you will end up in life. You make the choice to follow the path God has chosen for you or go down the road that has no set destination at your own risk.

While looking at the waves of the glorious body of water I live on, I sit here thinking what a strange thing it is that all the waves seem to look like they all flow in the same direction and make the same pattern of ripples along the moving body of water they share, yet the reality is that every wave and every ripple is not the same, and each and every one flow in their own individual pattern.

The most important thing about this realization is that no matter their individual pattern or direction of flow, these waves always reach the soft, warm sand somewhere because they always flow the way God has directed them to.

Don't believe that just because you share a similar trait or you are stopped at the same light, you are destined to follow the same journey. We all have the ability to choose for ourselves and to reach for God and learn our purpose in this life. So take in the positive moments that surround you on your journey, pick up the good pieces you were taught, and hold onto the positive attributes you were given. Be who you want to be, live for your happiness, and find the purpose that God has decided for you.

When the time comes and you are face-to-face with our Creator, what will you have to answer for? Will you have bestowed enough grace in this world to make your way into those pearly gates of heaven? Have you ever taken the time to think about your last day on this earth and what kind of legacy you will be leaving behind? How will you be remembered?

> The Lord is my shepherd; I shall not want. He maketh me to lie down in green pastures: he leadeth me beside the still waters. He restoreth my soul: he leadeth me in the paths of righteousness for his name's sake. Yea, though I walk through the valley of the shadow of death, I will fear no evil: for thou art with me; thy rod and thy staff they comfort me. Thou preparest a table before me in the presence of mine enemies: thou anoint my head with oil; my cup runneth over. Surely goodness and mercy shall follow me all the days of my life: and I will dwell in the house of the Lord forever. (Psalm 23)

This is what I know. This is what I believe. These words give me assurance and a sense of peace that I will one day find my place in paradise. These words remind me that we do not have to find finality, but that our lives can be everlasting if we only have faith in the Lord.

I have not been a perfect person in this life that the Lord has blessed me with, but I know that I have asked forgiveness for my sins, and I have vowed to work hard to never stray again from being everything that is right in the eyes of the Lord.

Suddenly, life seems shorter and shorter for all of us who are left living. The question is, will you let the world and life get the best of you and hinder you from living your best life, or will you challenge yourself to make this life everything you want it to be?

Will you decide to live the life you always wanted, or will you continue living a life of frustration and regret? Will you pursue your happiness and show your gratitude to the Lord so that your loved ones and others may see what it means to live a life of gratefulness, happiness, and joyous satisfaction?

Will you choose to live freely? Free of the burdens you can prevent, free of regret, free of anger and disappointment? Will you learn to reach for your perfect life and take ownership of it?

Don't just celebrate the holidays; celebrate every day. Celebrate the beauty that surrounds you every day. Celebrate everything you already have in your life. The people you love, the things you worked hard to achieve, and the friendships you have—cherish them all.

There will always be mishaps and bumps in the road. Take them on with a smile, find the positive within the negative, and do not let the hardships get the best of you.

Do not harbor resentment toward others or the past. Let go of all the bad, all the hatred, and let yourself truly live. Fulfill all your hopes and dreams. Be a force to be reckoned with and do not allow anything to change your direction, make you rethink your perspective, or destroy your beliefs that you will achieve. You can succeed.

Be the one who makes others see that they can succeed too. Be an inspiration and a beacon of hope for others. Find your faith and live your life knowing that the Lord will never you let you fall if you just believe.

> Though he fall, he shall not be utterly cast
> down: for the Lord upholdeth him with his hand.
> (Psalm 37:24)

Let your legacy be one that shines as bright as the sun, and when your time comes, make sure that you will know that in this life you won.

We must be proud and honored that we have been given the blessing to live. We must understand why we are chosen to live and learn to live for those very reasons. We must never allow the world to decide why we live and what living means to us.

> We live among the trees, the green grass,
> flowing waters, the singing birds, and the buzz-
> ing bees. We live! We live to feel the sun on our
> face, to be guided by the moon, to gaze toward

the prospects of outer space. We live. We live to feel the earth under our feet and the grains of sand surrounding our toes as we walk along the beach.

We live to give birth to the blessings we are chosen to carry; we live to find love that is worth the commitment to marry. We live! We live to feel each other within our arms and the Lord within our reach. We live to inspire and to teach. We live! We live to be afforded the choice to live life filled with hate, anger, and pain, or to live life filled with faith, hope, and love, giving us a reason to rejoice over and over again.

We live to smell the sweet, fresh air that we breathe each day. We live because God is allowing us to find our own way. We live! We live with a purpose you see, a devotion to determine what becomes of you and me. Will we choose the dark pits of hell or the glorious beauty of eternity?

We live, not because our mothers gave birth, but because the Lord believed in us and gave us His blessing to live on this earth. We are the chosen who are meant to achieve, to seek others and inspire them to believe.

The question I have is, Will you live burdened, or will you live free? I know what I choose, and I hope you make the same choice as me.

I choose to live and be free! I am choosing to rebuild the real me!

ABOUT THE AUTHOR

KLNelson is the author of two currently published books, *A Life Spiritually Guided by Faith, Daisies, and Sky Blue Pink* and *Beyond the Skies of Blue and Pink*, the stories of her life's path from the beginning, the loss she endured, and learning to keep living after loss. K. L. Nelson is a registered nurse and a mother of four men who have been her greatest inspiration in life. K. L. Nelson started writing books on her path to starting over and rediscovering who she really is all on her own. She is the author of the online blog *Kristabell's Ponders and Possibilities*, a freelance writer for the local paper in her hometown, and continues to be an avid believer in having the faith to let God take the wheel and steer you toward the greatest journeys of your life. What better way to continue on with her written works than to share with you how she is finding out who she is in her new book, *Can You See the Real Me?*